PENTATONIC PLUS

by Carl Culpepper

To access video visit:
www.halleonard.com/mylibrary

Enter Code
3288-5385-1506-2783

ISBN 978-1-5400-1364-4

HAL•LEONARD®

Copyright © 2019 by HAL LEONARD LLC
International Copyright Secured All Rights Reserved

Visit Hal Leonard Online at
www.halleonard.com

Contact us:
Hal Leonard
7777 West Bluemound Road
Milwaukee, WI 53213
Email: info@halleonard.com

In Europe, contact:
Hal Leonard Europe Limited
42 Wigmore Street
Marylebone, London, W1U 2RN
Email: info@halleonardeurope.com

In Australia, contact:
Hal Leonard Australia Pty. Ltd.
4 Lentara Court
Cheltenham, Victoria, 3192 Australia
Email: info@halleonard.com.au

CONTENTS

INTRODUCTION

In the brief tradition of electric guitar, the pathway to soloing and improvisation is typically initiated at the gates of the pentatonic scale. With its predominance of chord tones, the standard five-note scale—in both its major and minor modes—is easy to apply in a wide variety of situations. Additionally, the scale's two-note-per-string fingerings fall comfortably on the fretboard while outlining the familiar chord shapes. It's no wonder that most guitarists feel immediate gratification when they first employ this magical scale. Those first moments of experiencing a real harmonious connection between your intuitive ramblings along that box-shaped pattern over the song's structural palette can fuel a lifelong quest to express that unspoken yearning of the soul.

With the passing of time, however, the glory of those early days inevitably fades. Soon, you find yourself thinking there must be something more. Often, the young progressive-minded guitarist will strike out on new trails that promise to fulfill that need to expand his or her vocabulary. Indeed, the thorough study of diatonic harmony, including major and minor scales and their derivative modes, is an essential step in the acquisition of sufficient musical understanding. Even the time spent with the discovery of "exotic" scales, symmetrical scales, and atonal concepts can yield a harvest of new possibilities. But in the process, it's easy to find yourself in possession of a large collection of difficult-to-apply formulas and patterns. That storehouse of knowledge might be quite impressive to your friends, but what good is it if you struggle to make meaningful music with it?

Truth be told, even these sophisticated endeavors eventually lead most guitarists back to the basic principles of music. No matter how many formulas are memorized, or how much technical prowess is gained, the quality of musical creativity is still dependent upon the grasp of the ingredients of musical phrasing. And aside from the aspect of rhythm, there is nothing more fundamental to this concept than the relationship of the notes you play to the notes in the accompaniment. In a word: harmony.

It is with this simple realization that guitarists become aware of the need to tie things together with a pragmatic system of understanding. Lo and behold, you already have one, and you probably learned it at the outset of your musical quest. You guessed it—the pentatonic scale. That basic scale can work as a gateway to a higher level of capability (and even understanding) when it comes to phrasing vocabulary, no matter how musically advanced you have become. So, whether you're just getting started with lead guitar, or you're a pro player looking to rekindle or expand your creativity, I hope you'll find the concepts in this book/video helpful and inspiring as you explore the myriad possibilities that surround that familiar scale.

About the Video

Each chapter in this book includes a full video lesson. Timecodes are shown with each notated playing example in the book so you can jump right to the demonstration in the video. To stream or download the videos, simply visit **www.halleonard.com/mylibrary** and enter the code from page 1 of this book.

CLASSIC ROCK AND BLUES ROCK VARIATIONS

For almost a century now, the pentatonic and blues scale–based vocabulary has become fundamental to the fabric of music—especially improvised music. Whether you're just embarking on your path, or you're an accomplished shredder, the earlier phrasing style and applications of these scales will always bear review. If you are in the former category, make sure that you are familiar with the basic scale and a pattern or two (see Appendix, p. 37) before proceeding with the licks. If you already have that much down, you're ready to rock on.

Basic Scale Runs and Phrases

Let's start off with some simple ideas that make use of the pentatonic and blues scales in their basic designs without too much variation. Here is an Eric Clapton–inspired lick entirely composed of C minor pentatonic tones.

Fig. 1 (0:10)

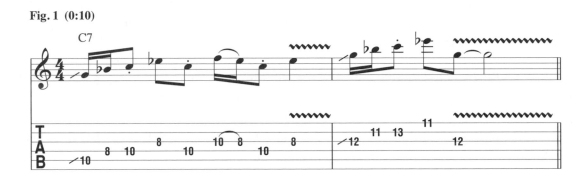

The austere C minor pentatonic scale evokes the classic blues sound when played against a variety of chord types. The minor 3rd (E♭) is the focal point of the line, both in pitch and rhythm. Notice that it falls on three of the four backbeats (beats 2 and 4), and it is the highest pitch in the run. This kind of accentuation of the minor sound has a profound effect on the impact of the phrase. Keep in mind that while these structural details are not typically consciously performed, they explain the effectiveness of an idea. Therefore, they are certainly worth considering while learning or creating concepts.

Combining Minor and Major Pentatonics

Major and minor pentatonic scales are often combined to shift the mood while playing over a single chord. In the next example, the phrasing begins by using the C major pentatonic to establish a connection to the underlying chord (or mood of the song) before moving into a darker mood with the minor pentatonic in the second half. While this particular phrase is a doff of the cap to Eric Clapton, you will find this a very common technique for varying the mood in pentatonic-based ideas.

Fig. 2 (2:44)

While learning the patterns for major and minor pentatonic scales, you'll find that they share the same fingerings from different locations on the neck. Notice that this lick simply connects the major position box pattern at the 5th fret to the minor position box pattern at the 8th fret. This makes for a very easy and intuitive method of achieving some variation in the mood without having to think of a complex change of fingerings.

> **Pro Tip**
>
> For a bluesy sound, you can use the minor 3rd against a major or dominant chord (For example: an E♭ note against a C7 chord). However, the major 3rd is not as easily applicable to minor chord contexts. In the minor context, the major 3rd can work as an unaccented passing tone, but proceed with caution.

The B.B. Box

No discussion of the essentials of pentatonic and blues scales is complete without the inclusion of the "B.B. Box." As per the name, this important variant of the pentatonic scale is most notably associated with blues guitar great B.B. King. The second half of the following example makes use of this scale.

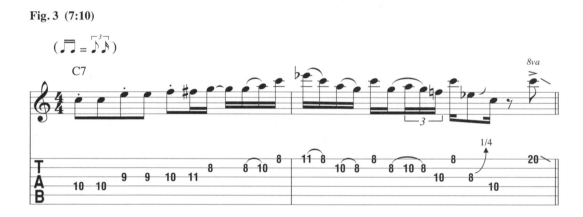

Fig. 3 (7:10)

When considered from the root C, this B.B. box scale could be thought of as a C minor pentatonic scale, only with a major 6th instead of a flat 7th (C–E♭–F–G–A). This brings out a distinctly more colorful mood than does the regular minor pentatonic scale. And, like the minor pentatonic scale, the B.B. box can be played intuitively over all three chords of a 12-bar blues.

Another correlation to notice here is that the B.B. box in C contains the same notes as the F dominant pentatonic scale, which is covered more thoroughly in its own section of this book.

Adding Tones to the Basic Scales

In the next example, the simple descending line utilizes the C blues scale with the major 3rd (E) added. You'll find this simple yet effective embellishment to the scale throughout the blues and classic rock spectrum.

Fig. 4 (10:01)

5

When played in the context of a C7 type chord or riff, the previous lick will evoke the moodiness of the blues scale, while sounding coherent with the chord harmony. The blues scale alone lacks the major 3rd of the chord, and while this is fine and well, it does not sound as strongly associated with an underlying chord which contains this note. Notice that the major 3rd is always played after the minor 3rd (E♭ or D♯). This is because the tension tone should resolve into the chord tone to be fully effective. While this is not without exception, the profound difference in the effect is important to remember.

Another important thing to remember is that including the major 3rd is effective only when applied to a major or dominant chord; it will not work well over a minor chord.

The major blues scale could be thought of as a major pentatonic scale with an added minor 3rd. In the following example, notice that the ascending line naturally has the minor 3rd tension tones (E♭) walking into the major 3rds (E).

Fig. 5 (12:31)

Note that each minor 3rd (E♭) falls on a weaker part of the beat than its resolution (E) in that lick, which amplifies the tension/resolution effect. You may also notice that the C major blues scale is the same fingering (or pattern) as the regular A blues scale. It is important, however, to make sure that you are thinking of it from the root of the scale it is played over (as a kind of C major), as this is how the ear will perceive it.

Major Pentatonic Scale

The major pentatonic scale has a distinctive sound that is often associated with country music, and, like the minor pentatonic, it provides a great reference point for expanding your phrasing. For example, in order to add a light amount of tension to the major tonality, the following lick incorporates the 4th degree (F) into an otherwise C major pentatonic line.

Fig. 6 (14:40)

This permutation was used extensively by Dickey Betts and the Allman Brothers Band. By adding the 4th, it's now only one note short of the full major scale. However, it can be a lot easier to improvise effective phrasing when you think of it from the perspective of adding to the pentatonic, rather than subtracting a note from the major scale. This is because the pentatonic scale is mostly composed of chord tones, and the chord tones are typically the "targets" in a phrase. In this particular example, the tension tone appears at the top of the ascent and on a couple of strong downbeats before resolving the line, thus making the tension/release concept more apparent.

More Combinations

If you take the concept of adding tones to the scale a bit further, you can arrive at the idea of creating scale runs that could be thought of as a combination of scales. In the following example, the combination of major pentatonic tones and blues scale tones creates a highly chromatic line in the style of players like Jimmy Herring and Steve Morse.

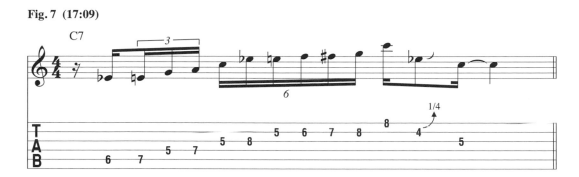

Fig. 7 (17:09)

This lick starts out much like the one in the major blues example. But notice how this line incorporates the additional note of F♯ (the tritone) from the C blues scale in beat 2. This results in a series of four consecutive semitones spanning from the ♭3 (E♭) to the 5th (G). The variety of tonal colors makes this simple ascending line far more interesting than a regular scale. When using this kind of chromaticism, it is important to make sure you are targeting strong tones for resolution, as you can see at the end of this phrase.

Classic Bending Variations

Among the many advantages within the pentatonic and blues scales is the ease with which you can apply the technique of string bending. For example, from the minor pentatonic, all the notes can be bent up a whole step to notes from the root's Dorian mode (1–2–♭3–4–5–6–♭7), which is the most common minor mode for music derived from blues. Specifically, in C minor pentatonic: C (1) bends up to D (2), E♭ (♭3) up to F (4), F (4) up to G (5), G (5) up to A (6), and B♭ (♭7) up to C (1). While this makes the pentatonic scale a great place to start, make sure to listen for the relationship between your target pitch and the music you're playing over.

Following is the kind of classic bending lick you'll find throughout the history of rock and blues guitar.

Fig. 8 (19:07)

This lick is essentially composed of two chord tones: the 5th (G) and the root (C). However, the bend from the 4th (F) is everything to the expression of the phrase. Make sure that you match the pitch of the bend accurately with the pitch of the fretted note that follows. The scoop into that target note is the heart of that howling sound we all know and love. Even in its most basic form here, this very lick can be heard in the playing of practically every blues-based guitarist ranging from Chuck Berry and Jimmy Page to Stevie Ray Vaughan and Joe Bonamassa.

Let's take that whole-step bend a bit further. Reminiscent of the style of Jimi Hendrix, the next example is an ascending line of unison bends that climbs the minor pentatonic scale.

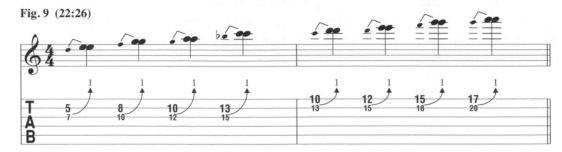

Fig. 9 (22:26)

The content of this line is simply that of an ascending pentatonic scale, but the expression provided by the bending and unison harmonies takes it to an entirely different place. Take the time to make sure each of the bends is in tune ("intonated") while learning this technique. The pairs of notes should ring true, with no out-of-tune "beating." Once you have that down, work on applying some vibrato to the bent note of each pair.

Here is a phrase that incorporates a whole-step bend on both the 2nd and 3rd strings.

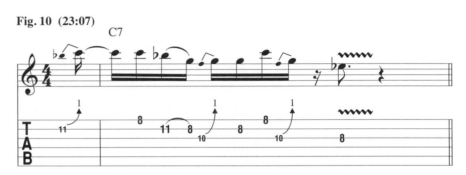

Fig. 10 (23:07)
C7

Again, make sure your bends are properly intonated. Starting on the 2nd string, the first note is bent to the pitch of the 1st-string note that follows, so there is a built-in reference for the pitch. Also, notice that the second group of 16th notes starts with our first bending phrase from this section. The last bend of the lick should stop abruptly, and with no audible release, before the final note.

This lick can easily be converted into a great repetitive phrase by simply omitting the ending note.

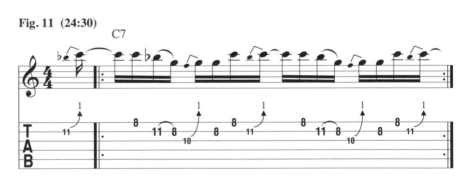

Fig. 11 (24:30)
C7

When playing the repetitive version of the lick, experiment with different fret-hand fingers in order to find what works best for you. Be careful with the rhythmic placement. The 2nd-string bend always anticipates the downbeat, while the 3rd-string bend is always on the downbeat.

In the next example, two bends on adjacent strings are played consecutively with the same finger.

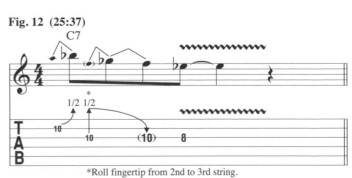

Fig. 12 (25:37)
C7

*Roll fingertip from 2nd to 3rd string.

This unusual technique requires that the finger used for the 2nd-string bend "rolls over" to the 3rd string (which is also bent) before releasing. Initially, the A is bent to B♭ on the 2nd string using the third finger. As soon as the note is bent to pitch, roll the tip of the finger over to grab the 3rd string. The 3rd string will be bent as a result of pushing the 2nd string up. The effect will be that of a pre-bend (or ghost bend), so you will only hear the release from that note. Since this is not the most precise way to effect a bend, the starting pitch of the second note is not entirely reliable. However, the overall expression of this phrase is a little more subjective than most—flavor at your discretion.

Double-Stop Bends

Single-string bends aren't the only ones available from this position—you'll also find some good double-stop bends. The first bar of the following example shows the basic bend that is then incorporated into a simple phrase.

Fig. 13 (26:50)

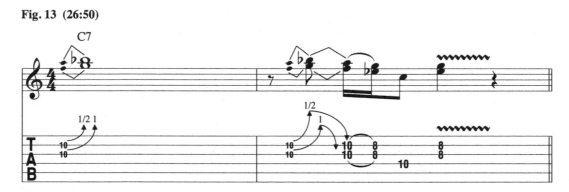

In this case, the two notes are bent up at different intervals. The 2nd-string A is bent to B♭, while the 3rd-string F is bent to G. Both tones are going up one scale degree, therefore they are moving in parallel. However, they are not perfectly parallel, since the lower note moves up a whole step, and the higher note moves up a half step. This can be achieved by using a separate finger for each string, or, more effectively, by laying one finger (usually the ring finger) across both. The difference in string tension between the 2nd and 3rd strings facilitates this without too much difficulty. Let your ear guide you. When playing over a C chord, the targets in our example will be the 5th and ♭7th.

Oblique Bends

In an oblique bend, one string is bent while one or more additional strings remain at a static pitch. The following example features a bend into a C major triad, set in the major pentatonic box for the key of C.

Fig. 14 (28:56)

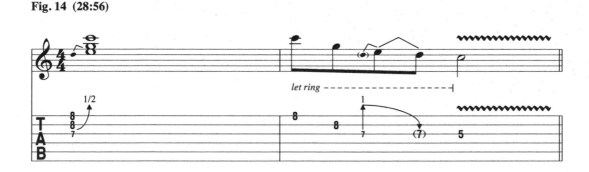

As shown in the first bar of the example, all three strings are struck simultaneously. Played in this straightforward manner, this simple expression is often used when playing over major chords. It can be especially handy for outlining a series of changing major chords that would otherwise be difficult to navigate on the fly. The 3rd-string D is immediately bent into the E. This alludes to the sound of the pedal steel guitar phrasing frequently heard in country music. The lick that follows takes this a step further by arpeggiating the tones in a simple descending phrase. Take care to bend the 3rd string in advance, as the pre-bend is crucial to the effect.

HARD ROCK AND
CLASSIC METAL PHRASING

The social unrest and cultural revolution of the mid-to-late 1960s ushered in a new era for rock 'n' roll. As a result of the need to express the angst of the times, a tide of louder, heavier, and darker music rolled in. Bands like Led Zeppelin and Black Sabbath appeared on the horizon, and even established bands like the Beatles and the Rolling Stones strove to push the boundaries of volume, tone, and emotion. While the musical expression of hard rock and classic metal was frequently more dramatic and even bombastic by comparison, the vocabulary still drew upon that familiar wellspring of pentatonic-derived phrasing of the classic blues and early rock era. Many of the ideas covered in the previous chapters are applicable to this hard-hitting style, and there are many more aggressive licks waiting to be had within the realm of pentatonic scales. Let's begin with a sample solo that incorporates licks and techniques both old and new.

Fig. 15 (0:00)

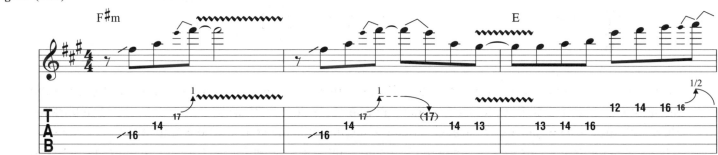

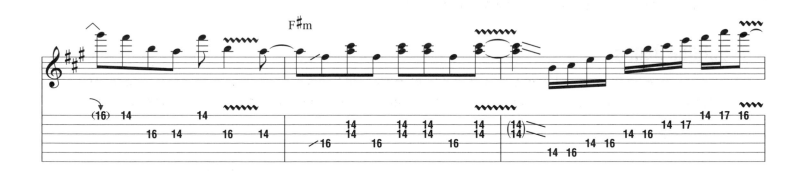

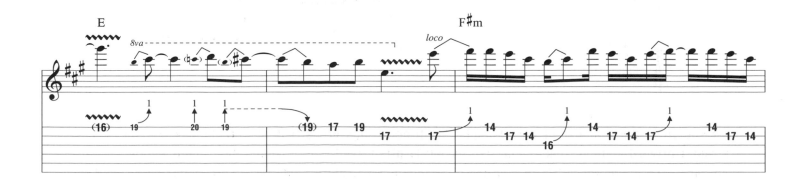

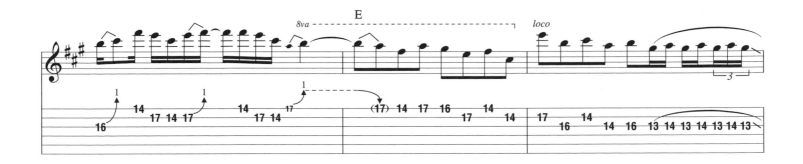

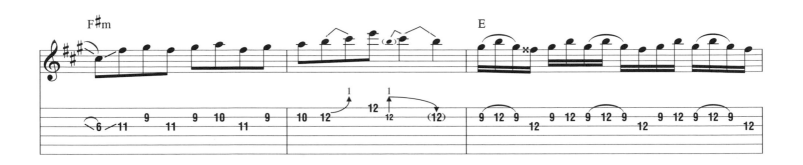

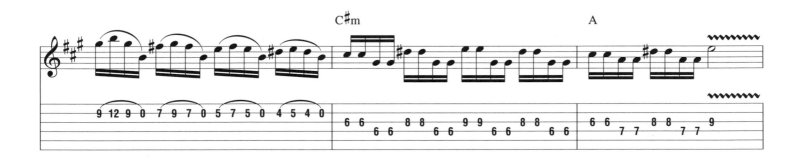

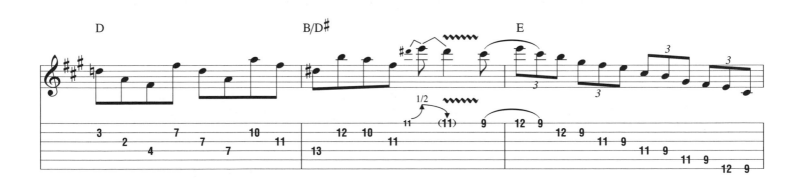

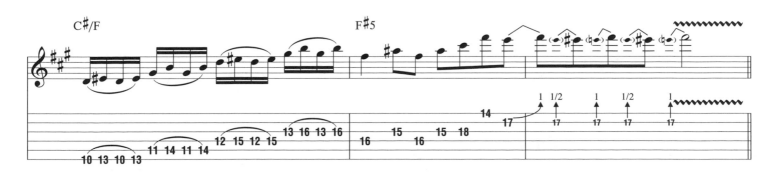

11

Basic Patterns

The licks and phrases in this lesson mostly draw from the familiar 12th-fret patterns for the E minor pentatonic and the E blues scales.

Fig. 16 – E minor pentatonic scale (0:53)

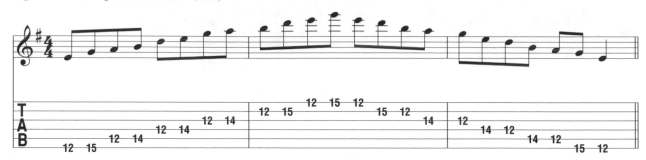

Fig. 17 – E blues scale (1:04)

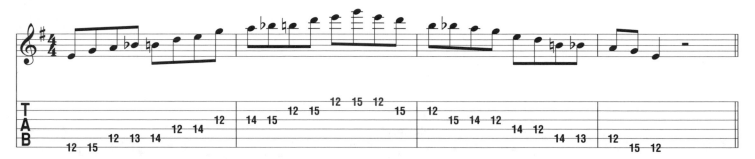

Bending Licks

The following line begins with a repetitive phrase that serves as the basis for the next few examples. The second bar begins with the Chuck Berry–style bend that you studied previously, before continuing down a minor- and blues-inflected scale passage reminiscent of hard rock/metal guitar legends Randy Rhoads and Michael Schenker.

Fig. 18 (1:24)

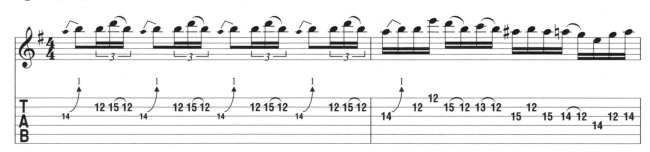

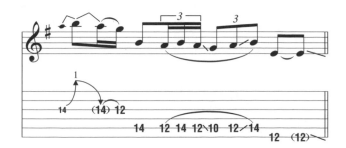

Before you proceed, take another quick look at that essential bending lick. At this point it is important to note that you can use it as a repeating phrase (as shown below) or as a part of the longer idea (as in the previous example).

Fig. 19 (2:39)

Another application of this lick is shown in the next example, where it is incorporated into a more complex idea.

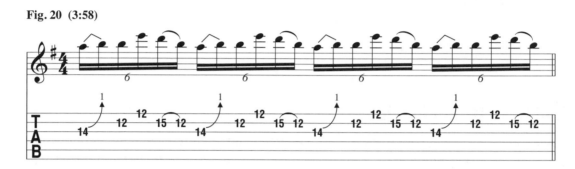

Fig. 20 (3:58)

In this variation, the original idea is expanded by the simple addition of the two notes on the 2nd string. The addition of the ♭7 (D) gives the lick a dash of extra color.

The next variant is slightly streamlined for speed. By omitting the high note (E), the picking difficulty is reduced enough to make the phrase easy to speed up. Make sure the first note of each group lands solidly on the downbeat, and the quintuplet rhythm will fall into place.

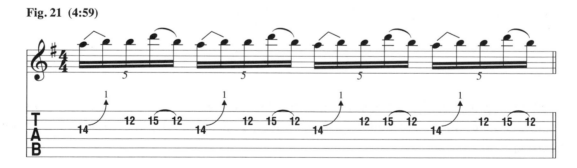

Fig. 21 (4:59)

Move the first two notes to the next higher string set, and you get another popular variation of this lick.

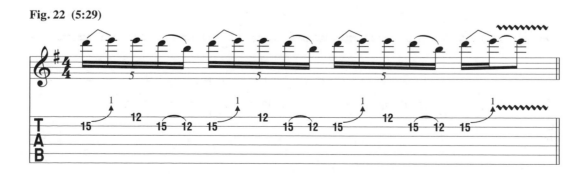

Fig. 22 (5:29)

And now, let's combine the two previous versions of the lick for a longer, more interesting phrase.

Fig. 23 (5:47)

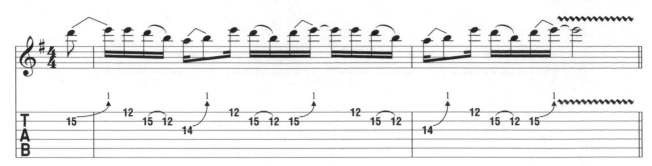

Note the new rhythmic pattern in this phrase. Since this combined version of the lick is a bit more complex, it holds up to a slightly more "in the pocket" rhythm. This is mainly achieved by anticipating the beat and taking just a bit more duration with each bend.

Repeating Licks Without Bends

Admit it: sometimes you really just want to burn. So when you need to kick it up a notch, you can play a phrase that forgoes string-bending in favor of a little extra speed. The following Gary Moore–inspired example makes use of the tritone (A♯/B♭) in place of the bend for a rapid-fire riff.

Fig. 24 (6:54)

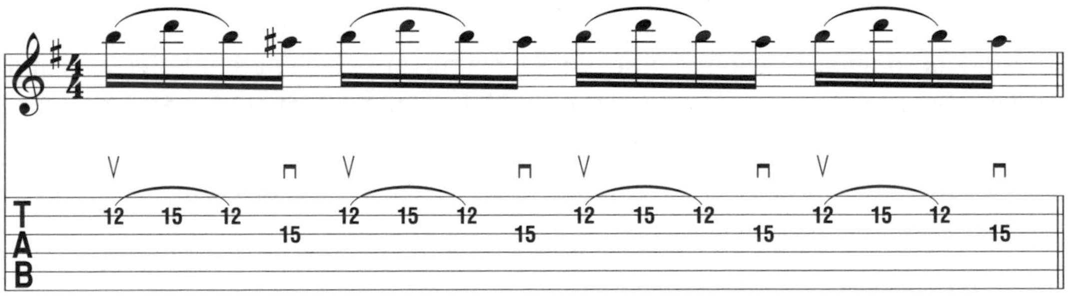

When played quickly and fluidly, this lower-neighbor tone can give the illusion of the note "scooping" in a way similar to a bend. Speed is aided by picking with an upstroke on the 2nd string and a downstroke on the 3rd string.

Let's take that idea a step further by adding an extra pair of notes in this variation.

Fig. 25 (7:55)

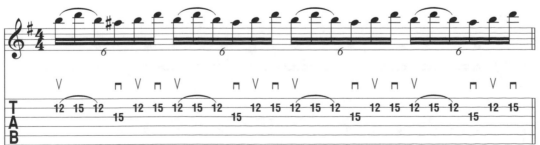

With these two extra tones, there are now six notes in each group. This can be helpful if you want to use this type of lick in a moderate tempo but retain a higher speed. When you start to build the tempo, focus on keeping that first note of the hammer-on/pull-off locked into the downbeat. And again, please follow the picking instructions to help you build the speed; it's an essential part of nailing these types of quick licks and keeping them in time.

You can also apply a straight 16th-note subdivision to these groups of six, which produces a phrase length of one-and-a-half beats. In addition to giving you a different way to subdivide (and therefore another applicable tempo range), this variation produces an extra element of rhythmic interest by "turning over" in the beat on repetition.

Fig. 26 (no video)

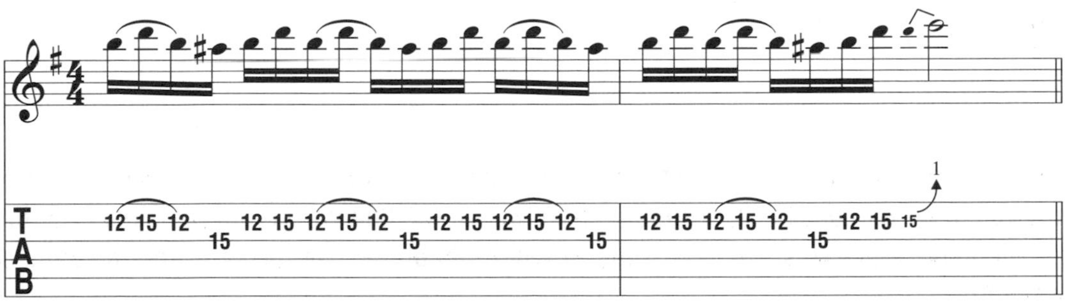

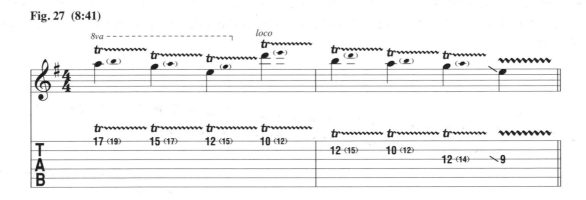

Trill and Tremolo

Trills and tremolo have long been a great way to ornament, or dress up, specific notes in a melody, but they can also make a strong statement in a solo. The following example shows this technique applied to a descending scale line in the manner of players like Gary Moore and Iron Maiden's Dave Murray.

Fig. 27 (8:41)

Notice that each main tone is rapidly alternated with its upper neighbor from the E minor pentatonic scale. The result is that some pairs are a whole step apart (technically, a trill), whereas others are a minor 3rd apart (technically, a tremolo). Pick only the first lower note of each set and rapidly hammer onto and pull off from the upper note. These slurs can be played in time, but most of the classic guitar heroes would do these as quickly as possible (with no regard to specific rhythmic subdivisions) when the music required major impact.

Scale Runs and Sequences

Rapid runs up or down the pentatonic scale can be tricky. The entire ascent in this Randy Rhoads–like line is picked.

Fig. 28 (10:30)

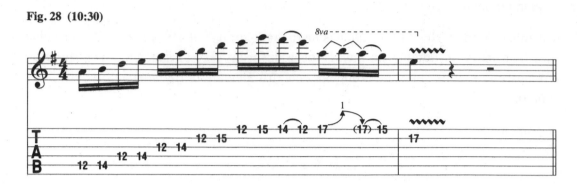

Alternate picking quickly across the standard two-note-per-string patterns usually requires some getting used to. To help expedite the process, try starting the line with a downstroke and then with an upstroke. Whichever way feels the most natural will probably be the best for you in terms of building speed and fluidity.

The F# on the "and" of beat 3 not only helps round out the timing, but also adds a little extra color to embellish the pentatonic nature of the line.

Scale Sequences

One of the best tools for creating longer lines in both improvised and composed solos is the scale sequence. A melodic sequence is simply a repeating idea that is carried through the key, starting on different notes. It could be only one repetition, or as many as you like. The example that follows illustrates one of the all-time classic sequences made famous by players like Jimi Hendrix, Jimmy Page, and Randy Rhoads.

Fig. 29 (13:30)

The first half of the previous example features an ascending sequence of three-note groups in triplet rhythm. Notice that the initial set of three notes (B–A–B) establishes a simple motif that is then repeated from each successive note in the pentatonic scale as the passage ascends. Notice too that the articulation of every first and third set of three notes begins with a pull-off. This little optional feature helps facilitate a smooth line by alleviating some picking difficulty.

In the second half of the example, a descending sequence is initiated with three notes in descending order (G–E–D). In turn, this idea is repeated with each successive note in descending order. Again, a slur—this time, a pull-off—starts every other set of three notes for increased fluidity.

Be sure to check out the next section on sequences for more on this topic.

PENTATONIC AND BLUES SCALE SEQUENCES

As I mentioned in the previous chapter, sequences are a great way to create longer lines in your solos. Repetition of your idea creates a cohesive sound, while its movement through the changing interval structure of the scale provides variety. Many guitarists focus their exploration of scale sequencing primarily on the diatonic scales. The strictly stepwise structure of a seven-note scale naturally lends itself to many of the common sequence types. However, as you will find in this chapter, the pentatonic and blues scales are surprisingly fertile ground for sequential ideas.

Fig. 30 (0:00)

Linear Sequences

Due to the layout of the two-note-per-string patterns, one of the most popular ways to sequence the pentatonic scale is the "groups of three" approach from the previous chapter. Although that remains a valid and useful sequence in its original form, let's freshen it up with a little variation.

Fig. 31 (0:38)

In the first half of this example, you ascend the E minor pentatonic scale while applying a descending three-note sequence to each note. Once you get to the top of the pattern, it turns around and you descend the pattern with ascending sets of three. This generates an interesting impression that the scale is falling back on itself as it progresses up or down. To give it a bit of attitude, accent the first note of each group. Experiment with the articulation and picking to come up with your own unique expression.

One favorite way to vary a sequence is to apply it in a cross-rhythm. A cross-rhythm is produced when the musical phrase is not lining up with the beat durations evenly. In this example, the cross-rhythm is a result of playing a three-note sequence in a four-note subdivision (16th notes). Therefore, it takes four cells of the sequence to get us back to starting on a downbeat.

Fig. 32 (4:06)

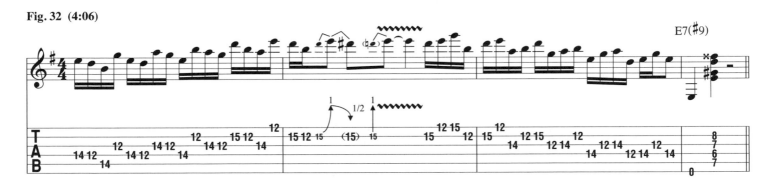

Now, let's take a look at a typical six-note sequence.

Fig. 33 (4:33)

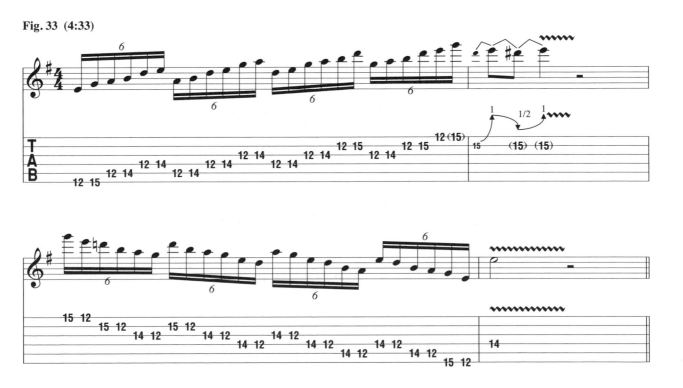

The previous example is a favorite for guitarists as it moves the sequence by starting on each new set of strings, rather than each note of the scale. For example, the second group of the ascending pattern starts on the 5th-string A, rather than the 6th-string G. The descending half follows this same precept. By keeping a consistent two-notes-per-string flow, the picking difficulty is dramatically reduced. You might find it helpful to work on repeating a single set of six notes in order to build speed. Try starting with both an upstroke and a downstroke. This can make a big difference in how easy it is to cross strings, depending upon how you move your picking hand.

As with the previous three-note sequence, the six-note sequence can be easily applied to a cross-rhythm.

Fig. 34 (7:05)

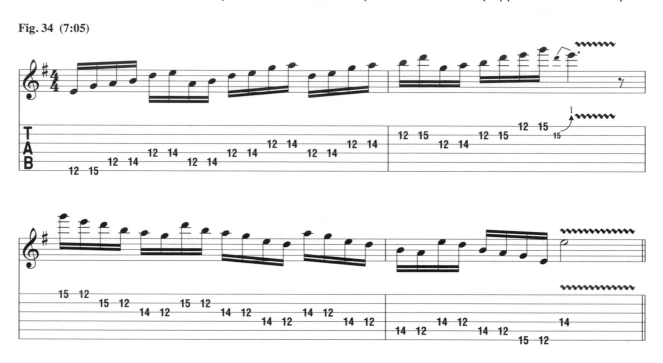

When played in a 16th-note rhythm, the six-note group takes up one-and-a-half beats. Notice that the second group of six starts on the "and" of beat 2, the third group begins on the downbeat of 4, and the fourth group on the "and" of beat 1 in measure 2.

The next example shows another way to arrange the fingering of groups of six.

Fig. 35 (7:33)

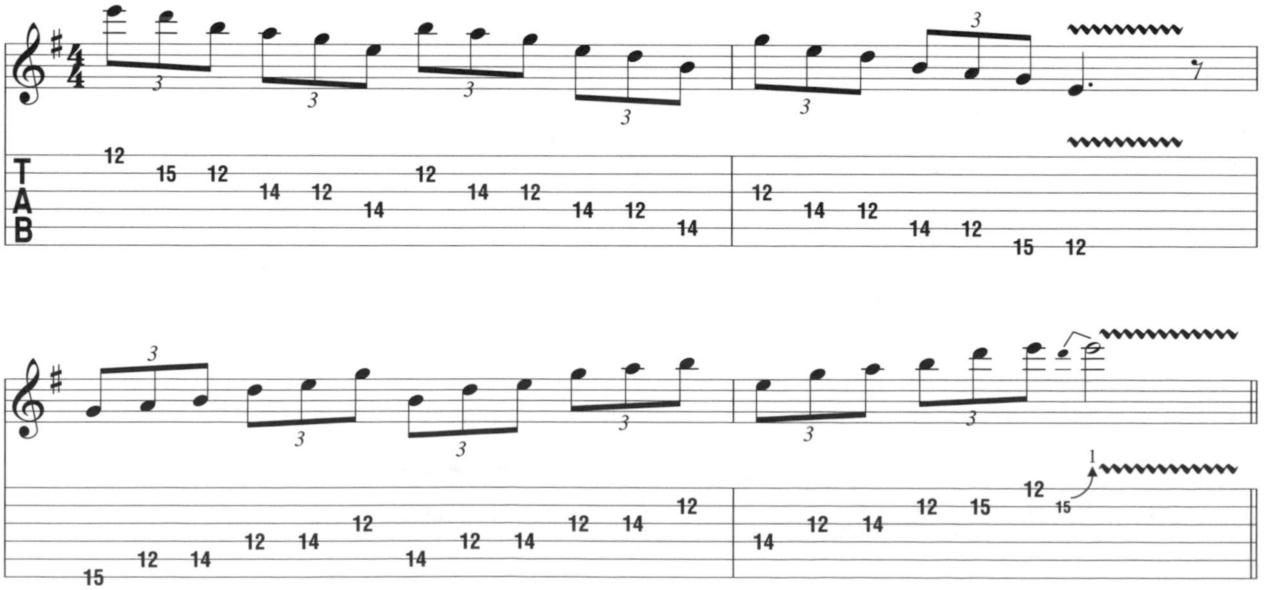

In the previous example, the phrase begins with a single note on the first string of the group. The change in the feel of picking across the strings in this somewhat irregular manner creates a very different groove to the lick. When playing these at higher speeds, you can also try to slur (hammer on or pull off) the last two notes for fluidity.

The following blues scale sequence takes advantage of the naturally recurring pattern in octaves.

Fig. 36 (9:45)

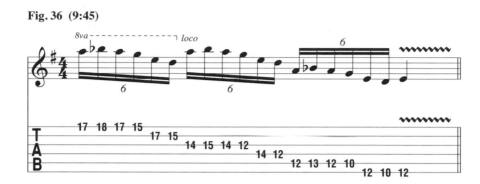

The repeating pivot of the 4th (A) and tritone (B♭) at the start of each phrase creates tension in the line, especially since the perfect 5th (B) is never played.

Sequences in groups of four can be quite a challenge within the standard two-notes-per-string pentatonic patterns. Some good solutions lie in moving laterally along the neck in order to alleviate some of the cross-string picking difficulties.

Fig. 37 (11:02)

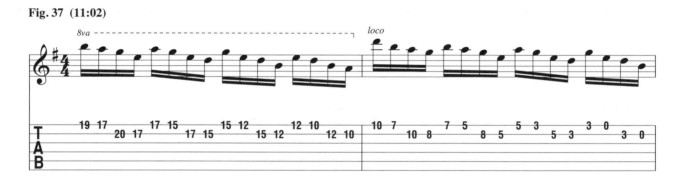

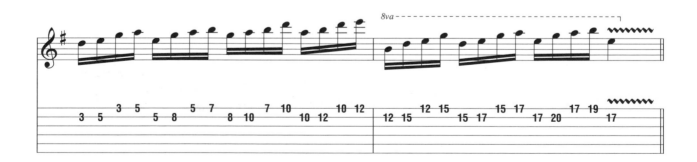

In this example, the picking is kept very consistent by moving the sequence along the top two strings. As with all of these sequence examples, experiment with starting on an upstroke versus a downstroke to see which works best for you. Take special care with the patterns that occur on beats 1 and 2 of the second bar (and beats 2 and 3 of the third bar). The irregularity of these fingerings can be tricky at a higher tempo.

In the next example, the same sequence has been re-fingered into a more compact region of the neck. By keeping the groups in two-notes-per-string fingerings, the picking difficulty remains fairly low. With sufficient practice, the position shifts and string crossings will eventually feel natural and reliable.

Fig. 38 (no video)

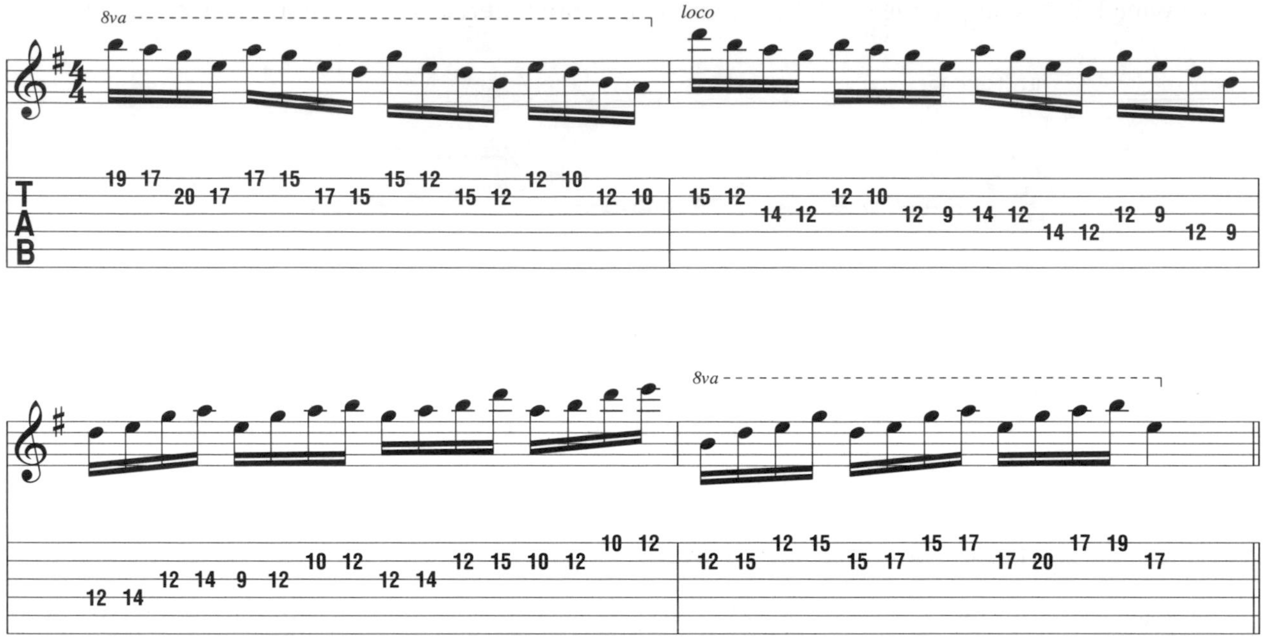

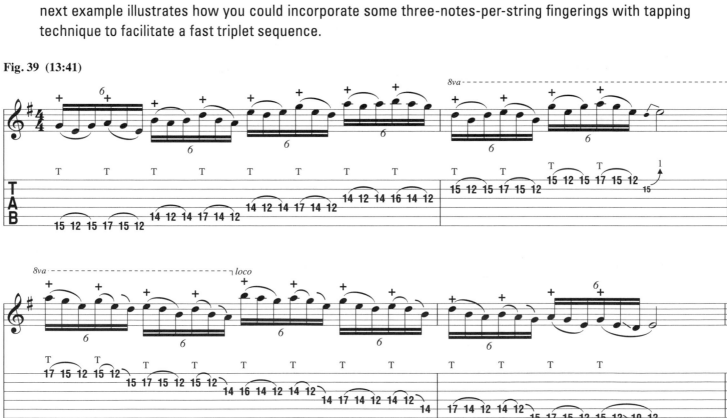

Sometimes it pays to think "outside the box" when playing fast sequences on the pentatonic scale. The next example illustrates how you could incorporate some three-notes-per-string fingerings with tapping technique to facilitate a fast triplet sequence.

Fig. 39 (13:41)

The ascending line in the first bar starts with a three-note fingering on the 6th string. However, notice that the first note (G) is tapped with the picking hand. After pulling off to the fret-hand index, the left-hand ring finger will hammer onto the G. The tapping hand then moves up to the A on the 6th string before pulling off back down to G then E. This formula is then repeated all the way up. The descending portion of the line is a straight sequence of threes. Take note that the fret hand has to "hammer on from nowhere" to the new string at the end of each set of six notes.

Other Linear Sequences

In addition to the "groups of ___" approach, there are many more possibilities of linear sequencing. In the next example, you will see a sequence that is composed of a short scalar line.

Fig. 40 (17:02)

The contour of this phrase is repeated from each new note of the scale by simply moving to the next pattern. As you might imagine, the possibilities for this kind of sequencing are virtually endless. The specific picking pattern is important to the execution of the lick. Make sure you spend the time to get it down.

Intervallic Sequences

Interval skips make a great resource for sequence ideas when a more angular sound is desired. Due to the fact that the pentatonic scale is already a bit more open than the diatonic scale, wide leaps in pitch are easily achieved. The following example makes use of a basic interval sequence that skips every other note of the scale.

Fig. 41 (20:35)

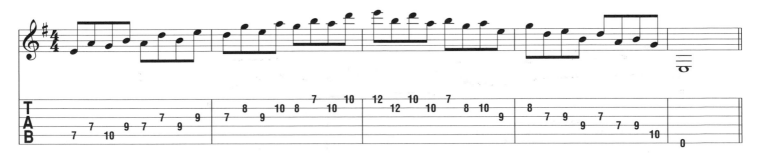

Applying this to the formula of the pentatonic scale results in a sequence that yields only one interval sequence (G–B) out of the five that is not a perfect 4th. While this is not a problem, it does seem to lack interest.

So in the next example, the sequence is set in a cross-rhythm to help generate the needed interest.

Fig. 42 (21:46)

Playing a two-note sequence in an eighth-note-triplet rhythm gives the impression that it becomes a "pairs of three sequence": low-high-low, high-low-high (and the reverse when descending). You can further obscure the pattern with variations of articulation (picking accents, hammers, pulls, etc.).

If you want to take it to yet another level, you can alternately invert each pair of notes while still using the triplet subdivision, as in this next example.

Fig. 43 (23:19)

If you have trouble with this one at the start, try playing it in straight eighth notes before trying the triplet timing. This will help you solidify the order of the patterns.

Let's take the concept of alternately inverted skips in cross-rhythm and apply it to a sequence of octaves in the pentatonic scale.

Fig. 44 (23:52)

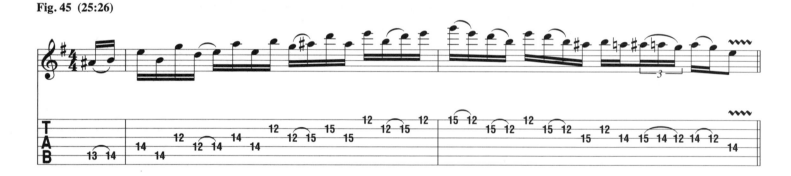

These wide-interval sequences are great at catching the ear. And, with all the string hopping, they make good practice for picking techniques, as well. Be sure to experiment by applying these concepts to any group of notes to create your own unusual sequences.

Mixing It Up with Sequences

Without something to break it up, even the most complex sequence can become predictable and uninteresting. Here's a short example in which ascending groups of five connect to descending groups of four.

Fig. 45 (25:26)

Notice that, in a couple of places, the tritone (A♯/B♭) replaces the 4th (A) to make the ascending sequence sound less predictable. On the descent, the groups of four are limited to only two cells before abandoning the sequence.

Just as it is with any musical phrase, context is everything when it comes to making a sequence work. Due to their very nature, the scale sequences presented here tend to work best as transitional or connective material. Once you have any sequence down, try connecting other ideas to create a cohesive musical journey.

Be sure to listen for the creative implementation of pentatonic and blues scale sequences in your favorite recorded music. For example, guitar greats such as Eric Johnson, Shawn Lane, Joe Bonamassa, and Paul Gilbert are among those known for their dazzling use of this device within their solos.

THE DOMINANT PENTATONIC SCALE

As you have seen thus far, the common major and minor pentatonic scales are generally applicable to most types of major and minor chords, respectively. They contain only chord tones and one or two additional auxiliary notes that are common to any of three modes. However, there are other pentatonic scales that are more specific. One of the most popular of these is the dominant pentatonic scale.

Fig. 46 (0:00)

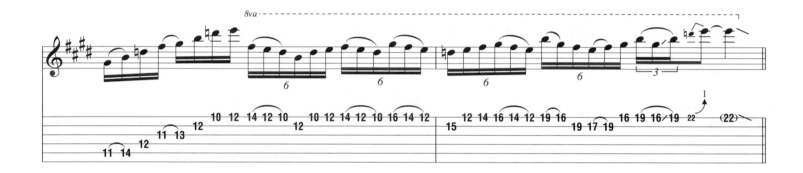

As the name implies, the dominant pentatonic scale is designed to fit the dominant chord (1–3–5–♭7), which is just a major chord (1–3–5) with an added ♭7th. For instance, an E7 chord contains the notes E, G♯, B, and D.

Though the regular major pentatonic scale works over this chord, it does not access the heart of its sound. What makes the dominant chord special is the relationship between the major 3rd and minor 7th (G♯ and D, in the key of E). The dominant pentatonic scale, which is spelled 1–2–3–5–♭7, does contain this combination of notes.

As you can see, the dominant pentatonic scale contains the chord tones of the dominant 7th chord, plus the 2nd. So if we recast the 2nd as the 9th, you can see that it's just a dominant 9th arpeggio (1–3–5–♭7–9) played as a scale.

Using E as the root note, the scale is spelled E–F♯–G♯–B–D.

This particular structure makes the dominant pentatonic scale very useful when you want to emphasize the dominant chord sound in your phrasing. Additionally, you can see that it is very similar to the major pentatonic scale. The only difference between E major pentatonic and E dominant pentatonic is that the former contains a C♯ (6th), while the latter contains a D (♭7th). For that reason, it is very easy to assimilate your existing pentatonic vocabulary into this new scale.

Fig. 47 – E dominant pentatonic scale (3:51)

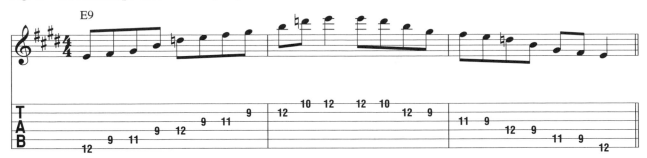

When working on these new patterns, make sure to pay attention to the sound. Although the difference to major pentatonic is only one note, it's a very meaningful change. A conscientious approach to training your ear to this adjustment will make a big difference in how well you can apply it.

The following example is a phrase from this chapter's intro solo. It makes use of open strings, lateral fingerings, and a pivot phrase to create a line that travels up the neck.

Fig. 48 (5:11)

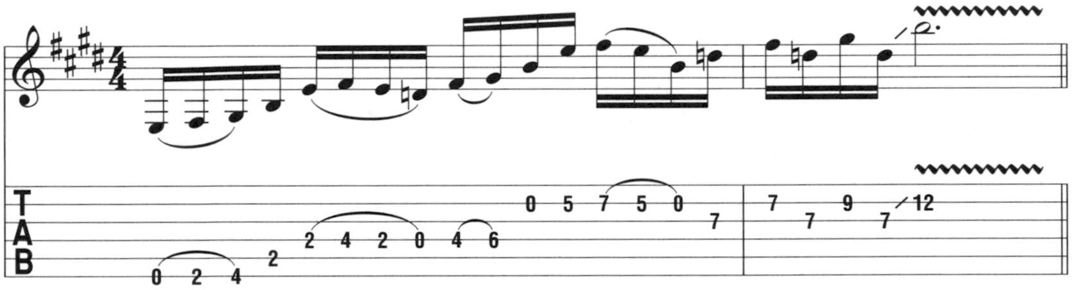

Starting with a scalar line, the use of open strings and pull-offs enables smooth transitions through the position shifts. Going into the second bar, the pivot off the D note drives home the dominant flavor.

The next example outlines a G♯m7(♭5) or half-diminished arpeggio, which is indigenous to the dominant pentatonic scale.

Fig. 49 – G♯m7(♭5) arpeggio (8:55)

Notice that the notes of the G♯m7(♭5) arpeggio (G♯–B–D–F♯) are the same notes as the E dominant pentatonic scale, or E9 chord, with the root (E) omitted. On a side note, blues players like Stevie Ray Vaughan will often play the m7(♭5) a major 3rd above the key's root as a substitute for a dominant chord—for example, G♯m7(♭5) for E7 or E9, and C♯m7(♭5) for A7 or A9.

Just as sequences can be applied to scales for interesting lines, they can also be applied to arpeggios. In this next example, a sequence is applied to G#m7(♭5).

Fig. 50 (9:46)

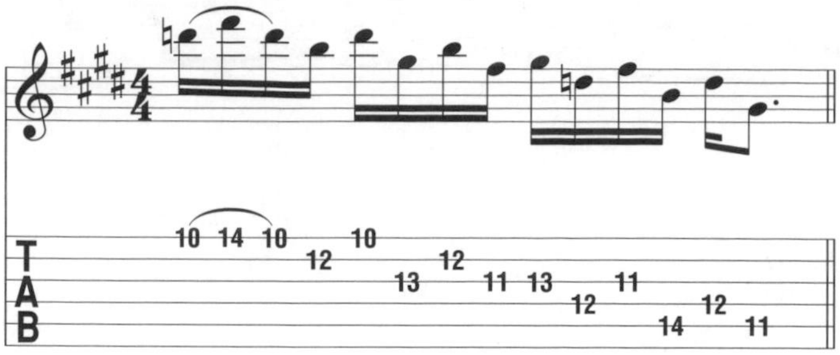

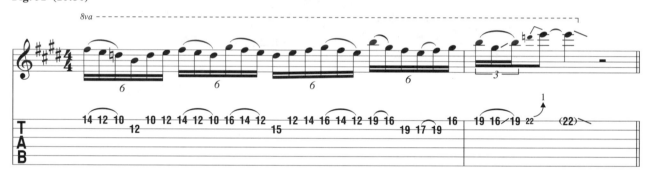

The design of this sequence is that of "backing up on itself" in a way that would be similar to a common scale sequence. The intervallic nature of an arpeggio will often make basic sequence concepts sound even more interesting.

In addition to the basic two-notes-per-string patterns, you can also arrange the notes in ways that create patterns with more lateral reach. The following phrase employs shapes along the top two strings that use three notes on a single string to facilitate the highly legato attack.

Fig. 51 (10:50)

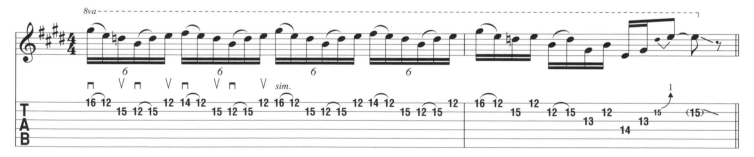

This shape not only lends itself to the articulation of pull-offs on the top string but also makes the alternate picking on the ascent of each phrase far easier. Start each of these ascending fragments with a downstroke. Note that at beat 4 of the first measure, the pattern changes and thus is fingered differently. Here, revert to a two-notes-per-string fingering.

The outro lick from the intro solo at the beginning of this chapter starts with this same kind of two-notes-per-string pattern, but this time in repetitive groups of six.

Fig. 52 (14:18)

The "shuffle picking" pattern is important to the articulation of the first measure, so be sure to follow the picking instructions above the tab. Notice the descending E7 arpeggio sequence in the second bar is the same kind of sequence used on the G#m7(♭5) arpeggio earlier.

THE DOMINANT 11 PENTATONIC SCALE

Another pentatonic variation that is applicable when playing over dominant chords is the dominant 11 pentatonic scale, also sometimes called the Indian pentatonic scale.

Fig. 53 (0:00)

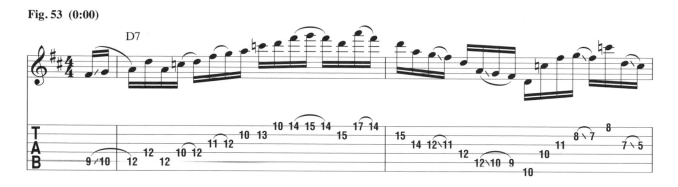

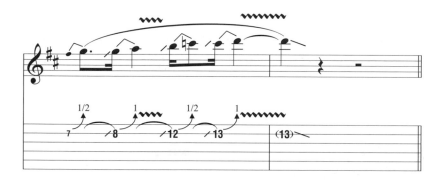

As you have seen in previous chapters, the pentatonic scales tend to contain chord tones and one or two auxiliary notes. The dominant 11 pentatonic scale is no exception, as it contains all the chord tones of a dominant 7th chord (1–3–5–♭7) plus the 4th (or 11th). So the scale spelling is 1–3–4–5–♭7.

If you look closely at that formula, you'll notice that the only difference between it and the minor pentatonic scale is the *major* 3rd. As you will see, any of the two-notes-per-string fingerings for dominant 11 pentatonic are easily derived from the minor pentatonic shapes.

To begin, let's play in the key of D (D–F♯–G–A–C), using a box pattern area derived from the popular root-position minor pentatonic shape.

Fig. 54 – D dominant 11 pentatonic scale (1:26)

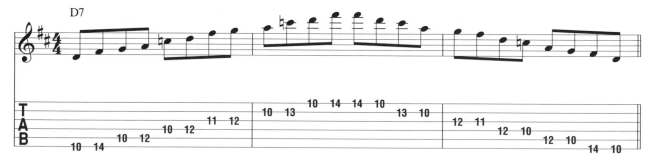

It should be easy to think of this pattern as originating from the D minor pentatonic box in the 10th position, but with the F notes raised to F♯. If you are already familiar with all the standard patterns for minor pentatonic, this will be an easy adjustment for each position.

Due to the unique arrangement of tones and how they fall across the fretboard, this scale lends itself to some handy diagonal fingerings by alternating two and three notes to a string.

Fig. 55 (3:40)

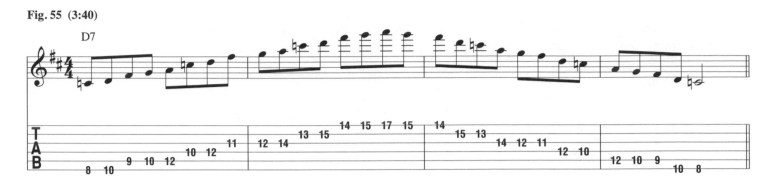

Notice that the pairs of strings (6–5, 4–3, 2–1) each contain all five notes of the scale. Therefore, the pattern simply repeats in octaves. In addition to facilitating quick runs, this kind of fingering can be handy for creating ideas that need to have consistent articulation across a wide range. Try starting patterns like this from any note of the scale.

Alternatively, the two-notes-per-string approach is great for phrasing that centers on a chord shape. In the following exercise, visualize the 10th-position D7 barre chord (or arpeggio) as you play through the pattern.

Fig. 56 (5:13)

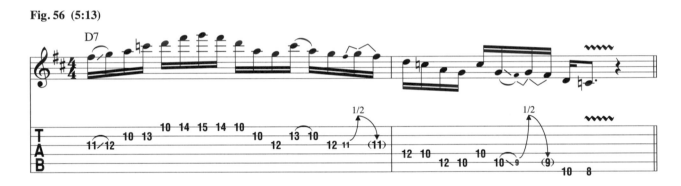

Notice that the half step between the 3rd and 4th degrees is prominently featured in this lick. Starting with a slide from F♯ to G, the line continues up one octave, turning around on the high G. The descending portion of the phrase includes two half-step bends, from F♯ to G, in two octaves as well. Take special care to bend accurately.

The diagonal fingering of the dominant 11 pentatonic scale is particularly useful for smooth articulation in quick runs. The following example is a variation on the classic "pentatonic threes" sequence that we saw in the Hard Rock and Classic Metal chapter.

Fig. 57 (7:51)

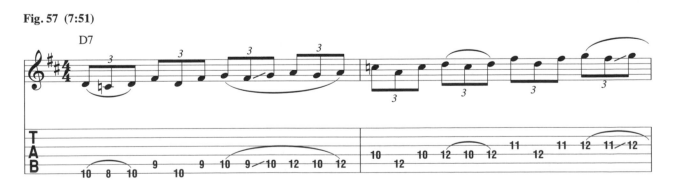

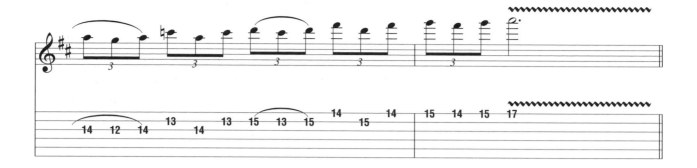

Having three notes on every other string makes it easy to apply more slurs (slides, hammer-ons, pull-offs) than you might be able to do in a standard two-notes-per-string pattern. Only the first two of seven consecutive notes on the 5th string are picked. The remaining notes are slurred: pull-off, slide, hammer-on, pull-off, hammer-on. This fluid combination is repeated in the next octave, on the 3rd string.

The diagonal phrase below is based on the connection of a couple of D major triad shapes.

Fig. 58 (11:33)

Here, the 4th (G) helps to make fluid connections between the octaves while bringing out this note's musical tension with the major 3rd (F#). The two successive index-finger slides on the 3rd string can be tricky, so practice for accuracy. For maximum effect, the ♭7 (C) is saved for the end of the phrase.

The notes of the dominant 11 pentatonic scale make it applicable to a wide variety of dominant chord and bluesy scenarios. One particularly fun use is over the V7 chord of a V7–i progression, including that which is found in a minor blues (D7 of a D7–Gm progression, e.g.). This next example shows how the scale works over a D7 chord.

Fig. 59 (14:09)

Freely

THE HIRAJOSHI SCALE

Along with the more commonplace pentatonic scales, there are many other ways in which one might arrange a five-note selection within an octave. Among those are some interesting and even exotic-sounding combinations, such as the Hirajoshi scale. This special pentatonic scale is often associated with the Japanese music of the koto, but it can be readily applied to a variety of rock-oriented scenarios to create some unusual yet compelling flavors.

Fig. 60 (0:00)

Moderately fast ♩ = 124

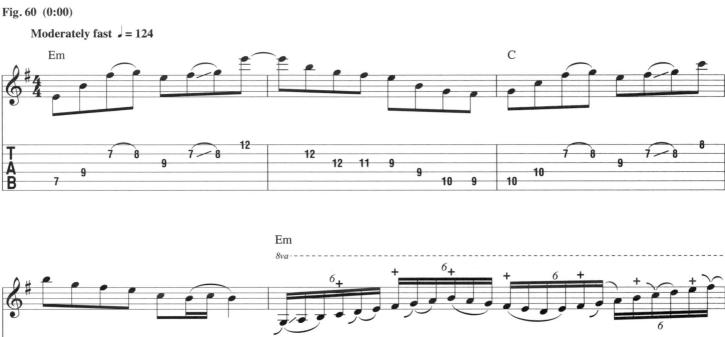

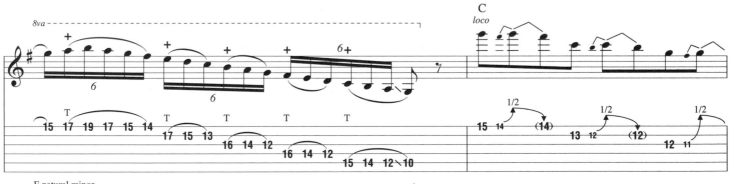

E natural minor

E natural minor

B Phrygian Dominant

There are a couple of elements that make the Hirajoshi scale sound noticeably different from the standard pentatonic patterns. Unlike the other pentatonic scales in this book, this one contains two semitones (half steps) within the octave. This creates a high degree of tension and color that has to be handled with intent. Let's look at the minor mode of Hirajoshi starting on E.

Fig. 61 – E Hirajoshi scale formula (2:24)

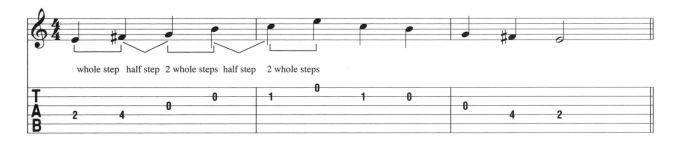

The minor mode of the Hirajoshi scale (1–2–♭3–5–♭6) contains the chord tones of a minor triad (1–♭3–5), along with a color tone (2) and a tension tone (♭6). Although these half steps make the Hirajoshi scale a bit less "user-friendly" than the standard pentatonic patterns, it facilitates exploring the natural tension and release that is required for effective phrasing.

Let's take a look at how we can finger this scale using a 6th-string root.

Fig. 62 – E Hirajoshi scale positional pattern (3:01)

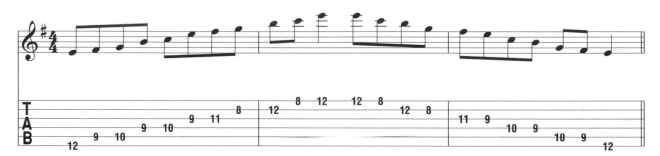

Like most pentatonic scales, the Hirajoshi can be adapted to a two-notes-per-string pattern. Pay special attention to the chord tones (arpeggio) within the overall shape—in this case, an Em arpeggio. In order to phrase effectively with the tension and color, you'll need to be able to resolve to chord tones when the music calls for it.

All five notes of the scale can be easily played on two strings (no stretches) with a combination of two notes on one string and three on another. This lends itself to some nice diagonal fingering possibilities. Take care to make smooth shifts between each five-note pattern.

Fig. 63 – E Hirajoshi scale diagonal pattern (4:32)

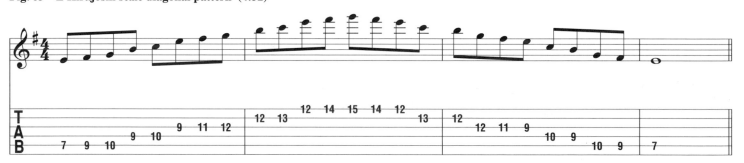

The Em(add9) arpeggio in the following example is inspired by the two-finger technique used by Django Reinhardt.

Fig. 64 (5:13)

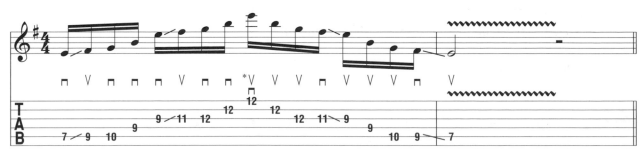

*Downstroke or upstroke

34

Notice that the ♭6th (C) in the previous example is simply omitted from the scale to create this arpeggio. It can be helpful to practice runs like this, and then try adding the tension note sparingly. Take special care when using the ♭6 over the tonic chord (in this key, Em), as it will require resolution to the 5th to be effective in most cases.

The irregular intervallic structure of the Hirajoshi scale makes it easy to create interesting linear phrases where the natural minor scale might normally be used.

Fig. 65 (7:10)

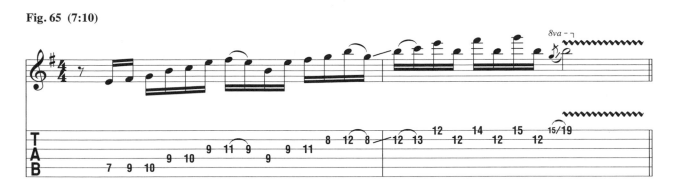

The ♭6th (C) provides a smattering of tension and flavor in the ascending portion of the phrase. The ending pivot lick relieves the tension by avoiding this note. Try to keep this concept in mind when creating your own runs with the Hirajoshi scale.

In the following repetitive lick, all five tones of the Hirajoshi scale are used.

Fig. 66 (8:43)

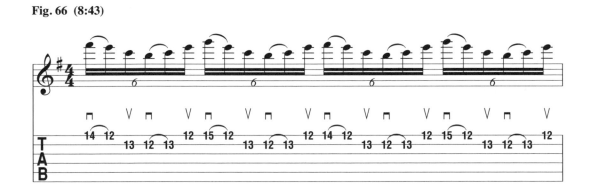

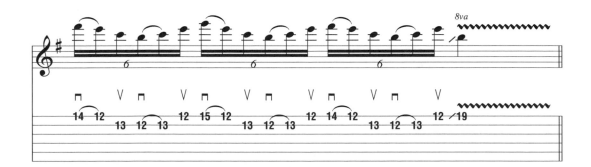

Although this lick uses the E Hirajoshi scale, it can easily be seen as a manipulation of the Cmaj7 arpeggio shape due to its focus on the C note. With that in mind, you might find it sounds more natural if played over a C chord rather than Em.

The repetitive idea below alternates between the color tone (F#) and the tension tone (C) for an intense flourish.

Fig. 67 (11:18)

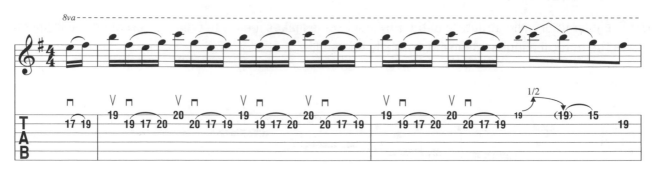

The execution of this lick makes use of the "hinge" barre technique in which the third finger hammers onto the 2nd-string F# and immediately barres across to the 1st-string B. As soon as the F# is struck on the descending half, the finger is "un-barred" in order to pull off to the E. This technique is then repeated in the next half of the phrase between the G and C notes. While this might seem like an awkward move at first, you'll soon find out why players like Marty Friedman and Jason Becker have favored this technique for a variety of blindingly quick licks.

APPENDIX

Scale Patterns

While the ever-popular box pattern of the standard pentatonic scale is a great starting point for aspiring lead guitarists, there is no need to stop there. The structure of most pentatonic scales will result in a number of very comfortable patterns when placed across the neck of the guitar, and all of them have their own inherent strengths and weaknesses with regards to phrasing.

This Appendix not only provides the basic pentatonic and blues patterns but also connects them with the basic major and minor chord within each position. These simple associations can be very beneficial in establishing reference points for fingerboard location and, eventually, note choice.

Major and Minor Pentatonic Patterns

Since the major and minor pentatonic scales share the same notes, and therefore, the same patterns (see the "Introduction to Pentatonic Theory" section of this Appendix), they are covered together here. If you're already familiar with the CAGED system for the diatonic scale patterns, you will see that the pentatonic patterns correspond exactly as you would expect. But this not a prerequisite for study here, and the information in this lesson can help prepare you for future study of diatonic scales.

For your reference, each scale pattern (with the major and minor roots annotated) is aligned with its associated major and minor chord shapes. Make sure to visualize the major chord shape, starting with the location of the root notes (diamond shapes), within the pattern when conceptualizing the scale as a major sound. If you have access to a looper or portable recorder (or a friend), try playing through the scale against the major chord in the background. Train your ear to relate each note of the scale to the harmony of the chord. Repeat this process against a minor chord in the background while visualizing the minor chord and its root notes (square shapes) within the pattern. Remember to keep your ear alert for the changes in relationships for all the notes.

Pattern 1 (1:19)
Let's start with the familiar box pattern, along with the basic tonic chords for major and minor:

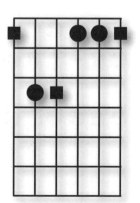

◆ = Major root
■ = Minor root

As you already know, whether in open position or fully fretted on the neck, this is the most commonly used shape. The physical placement of certain tones—including 6th-string roots for both modes and a "bend-able" color tone (4th of the minor scale, 2nd of the major scale) on the 3rd string—makes this the obvious starting point for most guitarists. As a matter of fact, even the most advanced players tend to use this as the hub for many of their fretboard excursions. The accompanying video begins with this pattern in the open position; be sure to watch the end of the segment to see the fully fretted position.

Pattern 2 (2:07)

The second pattern is another popular shape, as it is often connected to the previous shape for short scale runs. Additionally, the popular major barre chord shape is easily visualized within the pattern.

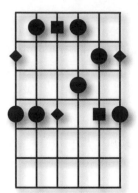  

The highest note in this position is the next octave of the "bendable" color tone from the previous pattern. Notice how the change of "physiology" in this pattern will inspire different phrasing and expression from that of the first pattern. While the minor chord reference in this position might not seem as strong as some of the other patterns, there is a wealth of phrasing opportunity to be had in this position. Be sure to take the time to familiarize yourself with it as a resource for both major and minor modes.

Pattern 3 (3:20)

The third pattern of the pentatonic scale is typically less familiar for many guitarists—all the more reason to study it thoroughly.

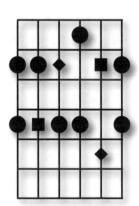  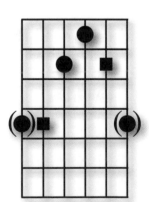

The major and minor chord shapes in this position are a little less comfortable than others—especially when including the lower string portions. As a result, many guitarists neglect to explore this region. You might find that the location of some of your favorite articulations (e.g., bending) are less useable in this pattern; however, this should be an excellent motivator for breaking stock, over-employed habits. Stick with it!

Pattern 4 (4:28)

Second place for most popular pentatonic shape has to be the fourth pattern.

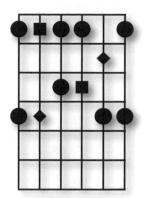 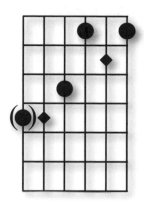 

Just as the 5th-string root barre chord shapes are almost as favored as their 6th-string counterparts, and so is the pentatonic pattern found in this position. This pattern is easily visualized as it bears close resemblance to the first pattern, simply moved over by one string. Here, the color tone is played by the third or fourth finger on the 2nd string, thus facilitating easy bending.

Pattern 5 (5:26)

The fifth and final pentatonic pattern is another easily memorized box-like shape. Notice that the fingerings are laid out in pairs.

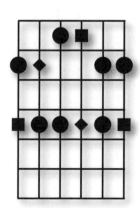  

Though the simple shape of this pattern is ideal for unadorned scale runs, you might find it a bit less intuitive for phrasing. As you work through the position, it can be very helpful to establish the connections with its neighboring patterns—particularly the adjacent upper-octave Pattern 1.

Exploring these connections will assist in a more complete view of the fretboard as you tie it all together. Additionally, the process is made much more enjoyable and creative if you are exploring real musical ideas. Be sure to review all the musical examples from this book and video, giving special attention to how the logic of any particular pattern affects phrasing and expression.

Blues Scale Patterns

Learning the blues scale patterns can be as simple as adding the "blue notes" (see the "Introduction to Pentatonic Theory" section of this Appendix for further explanation) to the pentatonic patterns. Like the pentatonic scale, the blues scale has both a major and minor mode. Therefore, each of the following blues scale patterns will have the same association with the major and minor chord shapes that you learned in the previous section. Be sure to review the respective chords for each pattern if needed.

Pattern 1 (1:15)

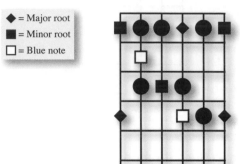

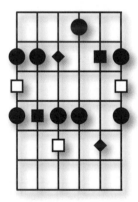

Pattern 2 (2:32)

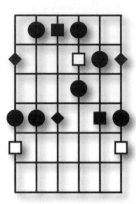

Pattern 3 (3:32)

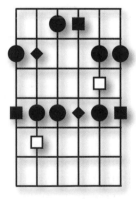

Pattern 4 (4:38)

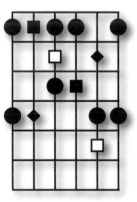

Pattern 5 (5:43)

You might find that the placement of the blue notes can change the comfort level of a pattern significantly. Be sure to experiment with moving any note to the next string up or down in order to facilitate the sound and feel you desire (watch the video for this segment). Any scale can be fingered in many different ways. The goal here is to give you a practical set of reference points and the building blocks to assemble a more complete fretboard concept. The sky is the limit when you begin to explore the options and think "outside the box."

Dominant Pentatonic Patterns

The two-notes-per-string patterns for the dominant pentatonic scale can be seen as a slight alteration of the major mode of the pentatonic scale. The difference being the dominant pentatonic includes the ♭7th in place of the major 6th. For example, in the key of G, the note F (♭7th) replaces of the note E (6th). Again, keep each position's associated major chord shape in mind as you learn the pattern.

Pattern 1 (1:11)

Pattern 2 (1:39)

Pattern 3 (2:30)

Pattern 4 (3:19)

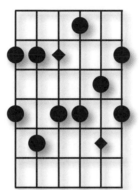

Pattern 5 (4:23)

In the same way that the addition of the blue notes can alter the comfort level of the pentatonic patterns, so can the swapping of a single note. Once you've spent some time developing a comfort level with these patterns, try coming up with different ways to finger them in order to achieve the expression you desire. In the accompanying video for the Dominant Pentatonic Scale chapter, you'll see some ideas for crossing the neck in a more lateral fashion.

Dominant 11 Pentatonic Patterns

Due to its intervallic structure, the fingerings for the dominant 11 pentatonic scale (also known as the "Indian scale") can seem unusual—or even awkward—at first. But, with a little examination, you will see that this scale is only one-note-per-octave different from the standard dominant pentatonic.

The dominant 11 pentatonic contains the 4th degree (as a chord extension, it is referred to as an 11th, hence the name) of the key and has no 2nd degree (which is included in the standard dominant pentatonic).

Pattern 1 (7:22)

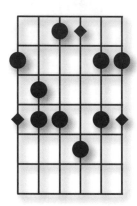

Pattern 2 (8:19)

Pattern 3 (9:20)

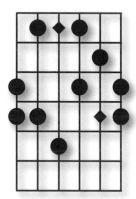

Pattern 4 (10:06)

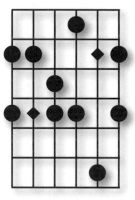

Pattern 5 (11:13)

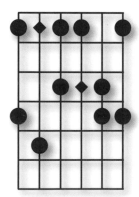

Though the comparison of the dominant 11 pentatonic shapes to those of the standard dominant pentatonic is a very logical starting point, you might find it a bit easier to compare these shapes to the minor pentatonic. For example, here's the G dominant 11 pentatonic at the 3rd fret compared to the G minor pentatonic scale in the same position:

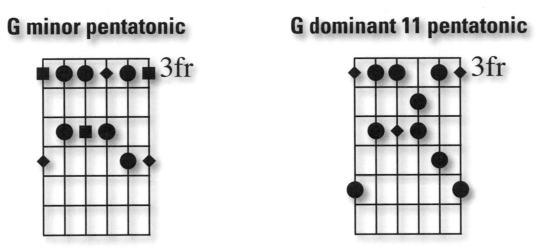

G minor pentatonic   **G dominant 11 pentatonic**

As you can see, the only difference is that the ♭3rd (B♭) of the minor pentatonic has been raised to a major 3rd (B) in the dominant 11 pentatonic.

By employing this process, we can derive the dominant 11 pentatonic patterns from the minor pentatonic patterns as follows:

Minor pentatonic scale			Dominant 11 pentatonic scale
Pattern 1	➡ swap minor 3rds for major 3rds ➡		Pattern 2
Pattern 2	➡ swap minor 3rds for major 3rds ➡		Pattern 3
Pattern 3	➡ swap minor 3rds for major 3rds ➡		Pattern 4
Pattern 4	➡ swap minor 3rds for major 3rds ➡		Pattern 5
Pattern 5	➡ swap minor 3rds for major 3rds ➡		Pattern 1

Not only is this relationship helpful in learning the patterns, it can also help with bluesy applications of the dominant 11 pentatonic scale. This is due to the fact that guitarists often mix major and minor 3rds in blues phrasing. See the video lesson for the Classic Rock and Blues Rock Variations chapter for ideas on blending the major and minor sounds.

Hirajoshi Scale Patterns

In various music theory texts of the western world, there has been some disagreement as to which mode of this scale is to be referred to as the *official* Hirajoshi scale. For the purposes of this book, the major-sounding version (1–3–#4–5–7) is drawn from the Lydian mode, and the minor version (1–2–♭3–5–♭6) from the Aeolian mode. Be sure to check out the Hirajoshi Scale chapter and video to better understand the theory behind it.

Though the Hirajoshi scale could be viewed as the parallel minor of the major pentatonic, its intervallic structure creates a much more angular set of patterns when applied to the two-notes-per-string system; specifically, it's the combination of the two half-step intervals with larger leaps. In spite of this challenge, it is still worthwhile to investigate the two-notes-per-string patterns of the scale.

Pattern 1 (13:26)

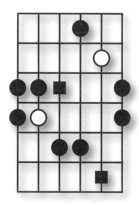

Pattern 2 (14:18)

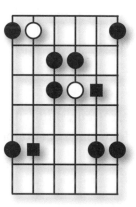

Pattern 3 (15:02)

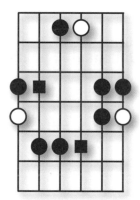

Pattern 4 (15:35)

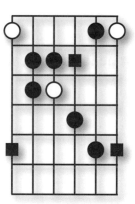

Pattern 5 (16:14)

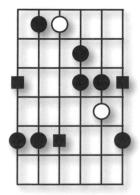

Introduction to Pentatonic Theory

Major Pentatonic

The familiar major pentatonic scale formula (1–2–3–5–6) can be used for soloing over most major chords indigenous to diatonic harmony. As shown below, these five degrees are found within all three major modes, which makes it a "safe" choice when soloing in major keys.

Ionian/Major:	1–2–3–4–5–6–7	(in G: G–A–B–C–D–E–F♯)
Lydian:	1–2–3–♯4–5–6–7	(in G: G–A–B–C♯–D–E–F♯)
Mixolydian:	1–2–3–4–5–6–♭7	(in G: G–A–B–C–D–E–F)

By the same token, it does not utilize the specific combination of tones that defines the mood or function of the modal context. You only get the major chord tones (root, 3rd, 5th) and the two auxiliary tones (2nd and 6th) that complement all three major modes.

Minor Pentatonic

Like the major pentatonic, the minor pentatonic scale formula (1–♭3–4–5–♭7) can be used in soloing over most minor chords indigenous to diatonic harmony. Again, it is a very "safe" choice and the perfect place to start when soloing over minor chords.

Likewise, the five degrees of the minor pentatonic scale (1–♭3–4–5–♭7) appear in all three of the diatonic minor modes:

Aeolian:	1–2–♭3–4–5–♭6–♭7	(in E: E–F♯–G–A–B–C–D)
Dorian:	1–2–♭3–4–5–6–♭7	(in E: E–F♯–G–A–B–C♯–D)
Phrygian:	1–♭2–♭3–4–5–♭6–♭7	(in E: E–F–G–A–B–C–D)

Since you are only using tones that are common to all three modes, you are accessing a generally descriptive minor sound with the minor pentatonic scale. It contains the chord tones (root, ♭3rd, 5th) and two auxiliary tones (4th and ♭7th). Under many circumstances, the ♭7th is also considered a chord tone. In such cases, the minor pentatonic is only adding one extra note, the 4th.

Relativity

Notice that the G major pentatonic contains the same tones as E minor pentatonic. Therefore, the two scales also share all the same fingering patterns. This is the same major-to-relative-minor relationship found in diatonic harmony, where the relative minor is found starting on the 6th degree of the seven-note major scale (four-and-a-half steps above or one-and-a-half steps below the root of the major scale). Though the study of diatonic harmony is not a prerequisite to the lessons in this book, you can let these points be food for thought whenever you encounter the theoretical concepts in this text.

Superimposition of Pentatonic Scales

The diatonic notes omitted from the pentatonic formula present another possibility in application: superimposition. This is simply using a different pentatonic scale in order to access the tones of a desired mode. For example, you can use A major pentatonic (A–B–C♯–E–F♯) over a G chord to get a G Lydian (G–A–B–C♯–D–E–F♯) sound.

Likewise, superimposition of a different minor pentatonic scale can evoke a different mode. For example, F♯ minor pentatonic (F♯–A–B–C♯–E) could be used to bring out an E Dorian (E–F♯–G–A–B–C♯–D) sound when played over an Em chord, since the color tones of E Dorian (F♯ and C♯) are present in the F♯ minor pentatonic scale. In this way, you can use pentatonic scales for more specific modal phrasing than is otherwise achieved by only playing pentatonic scales from the root of the chord.

Here are some of the possibilities when using superimposition with their related chord types.

Chord Type: maj7
Typical Scale Choice: Major/Ionian mode
Superimposition Ideas:

Major pentatonic from the root, 4th, 5th

Minor pentatonic from the 2nd, 3rd, 6th

Dominant pentatonic from the 5th

Dominant 11 pentatonic from the 5th

Chord Type: maj7♯11
Typical Scale Choice: Major scale or Lydian mode
Superimposition Ideas:

Major pentatonic from the root, 2nd, 5th

Minor pentatonic from the 3rd, 6th, 7th

Dominant pentatonic from the 2nd

Dominant 11 pentatonic from the 2nd

Chord Type: dominant 7th
Typical Scale Choice: Mixolydian mode
Superimposition Ideas:

Major pentatonic from the root, 4th, ♭7th

Minor pentatonic from the 2nd, 5th, 6th

Dominant pentatonic from the root

Dominant 11 pentatonic from the root

Chord Type: dominant 7♭5
Typical Scale Choice: Lydian Dominant mode
Superimposition Ideas:

Major pentatonic from the root

Minor pentatonic from the 6th

Dominant pentatonic from the root, 2nd

Dominant 11 pentatonic from the 2nd

Chord Type: altered 7th (e.g., 7♭5(♭9))

Typical Scale Choice: Altered scale or Super Locrian mode

Superimposition Ideas:

Major pentatonic from the ♭5th

Minor pentatonic from the ♭3rd

Dominant pentatonic from the ♭5th and ♭6th

Dominant 11 pentatonic from the ♭6th

Chord Type: minor 7th

Typical Scale Choice: Dorian mode

Superimposition Ideas:

Minor pentatonic from the root, 2nd, 5th

Major pentatonic from the 3rd, 4th, ♭7th

Dominant pentatonic from the 4th, 5th (for minor-major 7th/melodic minor sound)

Dominant 11 pentatonic from the 4th, 5th (for minor-major 7th/melodic minor sound)

Chord Type: m7♭5

Typical Scale Choice: Locrian mode

Superimposition Ideas:

Minor pentatonic from the ♭3rd, 4th, ♭7th

Major pentatonic from the ♭2nd, ♭5th, ♭6th

Dominant pentatonic from the ♭6th, ♭7th (for Locrian/♮2 sound)

Dominant 11 pentatonic from the ♭6th, ♭7th (for Locrian/♮2 sound)

Tips for Use of Superimposition

Not all the examples presented will be equally useful or present obviously good phrases in every situation. And, even though these examples are all "inside" scales, many contain one or more dissonant tones; for example, the root and perfect 4th are somewhat tense tones when played against a major 7th chord. But by spending time with each scale, you will find effective ways to exploit the many possibilities and, hopefully, discover many more.

Conscientious study and practice will quickly take your phrasing into new territory. You can hear pentatonic superimpositions frequently employed by great guitarists like Eric Johnson, Joe Bonamassa, Jimmy Herring, and Scott Henderson, just to name a few. Make sure you listen for this phrasing technique in the music you love.

EPILOGUE

I hope you have gained some new perspective on the pentatonic scales with this book and video. The variety of stylistic phrasing, expressions, genres, and technical possibilities are far too expansive to encapsulate in one text, but it is my sincere wish that I've been able to offer a compelling perspective for fresh exploration of our old five-note friend. I have no doubt that you will create your own ear-pleasing results when you reconsider the common scale.